Letters of Loss

Natalie Hall

BookLeaf Publishing

India | USA | UK

Letters of Loss © 2023 Natalie Hall

All rights reserved.

No part of this publication may be
reproduced, stored in a retrieval system, or
transmitted, in any form or by any means,
electronic, mechanical, photocopying,
recording or otherwise, without the prior
written permission of the presenters.

Natalie Hall asserts the moral right to be
identified as author of this work.

Presentation by *BookLeaf Publishing*

Web: www.bookleafpub.com

E-mail: info@bookleafpub.com

ISBN:9789358313284

First edition 2023

DEDICATION

For JSH

1949 -2023

One

Consumed by grief
Time infinite yet too brief
Frozen and Burning
Broken and Yearning

Silence stretches boundless
Consolation hollow and useless
Silent and screaming
Awake and dreaming

Breathe
Breathe
Breathe

Step forward
Push onward
Surrounded by love
From those watching above

Two

Sadness lives here now
Etched into every surface
One day joy will return

Three

Heartache is our new constant companion
Only memories for comfort
Perpetual reminders of the future we lost
Enraged
Lost
Exhausted
Still loved
Still missed

Four

First to call in a crisis
Always ready with a plan
The most dependable man
How has it come to this?
Even now- disbelief...
Rage, Rage at the most cruel thief.

Five

'Grief comes in waves'
Not here.
Grief is raging, lashing, roaring flames
Burning my insides
Fuelled by bitter sobs and tears
No relief in the ebbing tides
Hollow and ashen in its wake
Limitless - fire rages and raves
Without pity or mercy - scorching the cliche
That grief comes in waves

Six

Feel everything and nothing
Without shame
Feel regret and relief
Without blame
Feel despair and the intangible
Without name
Feel comfort and terror
Now nothing is the same

Seven

How do you summarise a life in a page?
The trials, the triumphs, the tea and cake.
The trivial moments are what matter most
The ten course breakfast, finished with toast.

Seven tissues folded neatly in squares
A penny for luck
Means nothing to a stranger.
The gentle rituals in shreds
The record forever struck

Eight

Senseless loss of a gentle soul
Taken too soon from a loving family
Uprooted lives in disarray
Consolation in fond remembrance
Kindness to others a lasting legacy

Nine

9

Nothing
Undoes
My
Brokenness

Ten

Staring
Hopelessly out
Overwhelmed with
Crushing
Knowledge

Eleven

Another day passes
No closer to comprehension
Gut punches at every turn
Every corner holds bittersweet moments
Reminders of unimaginable loss

Twelve

Regret lingers heavy
Air thick with words unspoken
Choked emotion
Pushed down
Down
 Down
Too late now, chances missed

Thirteen

Grey days give way to black nights
Bitter winds and festive lights
Tears sting for absent friends
Longing and sadness never ends

Fourteen

Dry your eyes
All is well
Dad is here - safe in dreams

Fifteen

Left stranded in heartbreak
Only misery for company
Suspended, trapped, contorted by grief
Scorned and mocked by monotony

Sixteen

Exhausted by tears
Leaden limbs resist
Open wounds that never heal
Still, we must persist

Seventeen

Dread
Envy
Anguish
Despair

Eighteen

Grieve the years you have lost
Grieve the one you love most
Grieve the road not to be taken
Grieve the bond cruelly forsaken